CURRENT

Current

A. M. SIRIANO

EOE

2010

Columbus, Ohio

EOE Productions

Columbus, OH

For quotes, interviews or general information, please contact:

PUBLICRELATIONS@AMSIRIANO.COM

Cover art and design by the author.

ISBN: 978-0-578-00211-8

For Mom and Dad,
whose joined life of dedication to God and family
continues to be the soul of my existence

Table of Contents

Table of Contents (cont.)

Table of Contents (cont.)

Table of Contents (cont.)

Table of Contents (cont.)

The Boy

LOOK—my castle's there undone,
Its bearing light, and hardly brave
Enough to smile at ocean's wave,
Or stand up to the sun.

But worse for wear, to the castle there,
Is he, the boy, who looks like me—
Wild, untamed, and far too free.
For reason's sake, might not he spare

Me just this once, his deeds think out?
Is it not enough that wind and tide
Should strike at ego's distinctive pride?
No! A future's all a boy's to rout.

Upon the waves he comes aground,
Pretends to flout me for the sun;
And just when common sense seems won …
He kicks my castle down.

Look, it's late, I say, and when
Will I have time to set aright
What a childish fool can spoil by might?
How will I mold this house again?

The waters lap upon my hand
As I set out to build anew,
Thicker walls, and an ocean view,
Though sadly made of sand.

Set

HE was really very young—
Allowed the moon yet for the night—
When stopped for once from his brothers' play,
    He spied the orb in his sunlit day,
Which flipped the world from so great a height
That wonder rose up to his tongue—

He was really very young
    And too much like the eye that hung
About to watch his way.

The Trap

'TWAS hot and wet one summer day,
Two deadly foes stood sparring.
The boy called Terence had found his mark
With Michael's mind, a-jarring.
I'll not this psych, thought the waning Mike,
So he searched for best reply;
But the older boy, so awfully coy:
"I know you are, but what am I?"

Ah! thought Mike, he thinks I'm had,
This cad, who seems to right me;
I'll find a name with such a sting,
He'll ne'er again come fight me!
"Thou wretch!" screamed he, "Thou garbage slime!
One lower than the fly!"
But Terence, cold, yet smiling, saith:
"I know you are, but what am I?"

"Monkey, lizard, half-cooked gizzard,
Slug or worm or snail!
A dot, a spot, a stain, some rot
That crawls up from the pail!"
Yet, though Mike's face was hot with rage,
Though well of hope was dry,
The cool aberrance of master Terence:
"I know you are, but what am I?"

Now Mike is grizzled, ever rizzled,
While the other, mute, undaunted;
No insult spewed is not undone
With words of wit so flaunted.
Another strike the harried Mike
Prepares to meet this sly;
But before such word, baboon, is heard:
"I know you are but what am I?"

On torrid nights, when summer's lights
Have left the earth its drenching,
You may awake to some off sound,
A scream, perhaps, a wrenching—
This warning only, to ne'er repeat,
Lest you, too, go awry
Like boys entrapped, to answer, answer:
"I know you are, but what am I?"

Hopeless

SHE professed to love poetry,
And I thought to woo her with it.
Until she said, "Not yours."

In the Gym

THESE were Spartan girls—
Wild-hearted huntresses
    With sinewy thighs,
Fierce at play
    With no mind for sport—
Only to be watched.

Across the wide, wooden floor,
Against a lonesome block wall,
    I watched.

Indian Summer

FAIR creature! … but not so fair today,
For time, that brutal ravager, has wasted you away.
    (I would have been far kinder than he,
    Had you spent your days with me.)

In truth, my Indian queen—
Oh, yes, exotic was my queen upon that wistful lake!—
    My first true love: You must remain
    A beauty in this lovelorn brain.

Perhaps that is why our last embrace
Was lost in Aurora's ghostly light—then black, no trace.
    I thought to follow, our love to renew;
    But what would I now think of you?

Eyes still lovely, I would guess,
But brightness often fades to yellow with all the rest.
    Sorry!—but I haven't the capacity
    To be again what you once knew in me.

Shame? You speak it freely—
Or so I imagine, were you here—
    But if honesty works within,
    Admit it: your memory is of *him*,

Long gone, that boy—and just a boy, with wavy hair—

And eager lips: Stay!—memory, merciful, stay!
    Conjure up my Indian night
    And guard my Indian day!

Fair creature, creature once fair,
Delightfully fat—she spoke not, just sat,
    Waiting to be enrapt
    By love untapped

Between our adolescent shores—
And so we kissed, and kissed, and—yes—kissed!
    Indian kisses all, raging and warm—
    A summer storm—

Yes, a storm, you must remember, as do I:
Your dark, delicate face, flushed with passion,
    Hair entwined in heaven's light—
    Just for one alluring night.

Then upon that shore, we kissed our goodbyes,
And I turned from youth and those Indian eyes,
    That lovely skin, that long black braid—
    And watched Aurora fade.

Sea of Carmine

PAST the edge of forest
Lies a field
That hosts in midsummer
A rush of sudden bloom,
A sea of carmine,
Purple waves and
Crests of white.

I go there,
When winds are gentle,
To see your face.

Lips

SHE hovered above me for what seemed minutes,
Watching me with deep, black eyes,
Hiding triumph there, relishing command.
Her breath was warm and sweet,
Her tongue languishing and wet,
And rising about her the scent of rose and spice.
She began to brush her lips, almost a flutter,
Moth-like, against my skin,
Upon my nose, and to my eyes,
Across my cheek, and to my chin,
Until she finally rested all their thickness
Upon the whole of my mouth.
Then she waited.
I could not breathe.
I could not see.
I could only wonder how so simple a thing
Could summon all of heaven.

Form Again

SUCH is that beauty, who rives the ancient wound,
And enters in, a sweet infection,
Pulsing through these used and collapsèd veins
To drop me to the ground as knight to queen.

Buds are seen, and blissful flowers bloom,
And sentimental refrain resounds about me
As saint and angel prove this love is real,
Blessèd take on what is suddenly mine—

The form divine—in you a risky offer,
As here before me, all your gifts at once
In a goddess' pitying condescension,
Willing to sublimate what is dust.

Release you must—for none so simple remains
Within the realm of beauty's shadow
And carries on as stalwart man; instead
He shrivels, dies, reduced by celestial germ—

Becomes the worm. He cannot function thusly;
Repels the Spheric face and seeks the norm:
Spent go I, and hide my vapid shame,
To a cave, perhaps, among the broken men …

Form again, so craved!—another chance
Into that realm, the glimpse you once allowed
To a failed saint and a fallen angel,
Gnashing up from my obscurity.

Distant Shores

EVERY day Sondra leaves at noon to hide away,
Nestles in a break room where the windows face
The open fields. There she sits, lovely black and white,
No longer young, but holding on to ancient beauty
Like Nefertiti's daughter, full of sadness and longing
For something lost, long ago, on distant shores,
Where noble lovers wait and sons become kings.

Fool

LOVE turns somber men to fools
And foolish men to kings:
At your side, Sinéad,
I have been all this and more.

Rose and Berry

WE have tried to curb their passionate advance,
But truly nature has its own designs on beauty.
The rosebush, wild at heart, fills her love-tilled bed,
And coaxes firethorn from his domestic frame,
Drawing berried branches up through her domain,
And smugly blooms in pink delight,
And dares the other, come again.

World

FOR sake of love how quick to lacery!
But the ruse, the hunt, the game, beats the brush
That paints your beauty as more than flesh and blood.
I admit the allure, but surely you are less divine
Than your assembled cells can claim; nor you as "mine,"
Though such has been my vow by each effusive flood,
Rendering word beyond devout to rise above the crush—
O my despair! The ruin of fair hyperbole!

But, ah, Belinda, lying there—
    She soaks up bold idolatry
And soon remakes our world in love
    And sweet embroidery ...

Topiary

HER head's like a changing topiary—
You know, a sculptured garden, but hairy.

Over

THE moon fails me tonight.
Bright and bold in the afternoon—
Surely it might have stuck around
To work upon her heart.

If you'll recall, Marianne,
We made first love beneath that light;
Were she to stay, perhaps again
The clouds would part.

The Flowers

THE perfume you wear is supposed to remind me
    Of flowers.
But truthfully, the flowers remind me of you.
When I stroll by that bed I am hardly thinking
    Of *their* beauty or *their* scent.

Sound and Video

THERE in the page lies a crumpled tag
    Stopped hard at 431.
Might I assume sweet Harriett
    Could simply not go on?

The Motorola's up, I dream,
    As she reads languidly,
Barely hearing Maugham's fair words,
    For din of fast TV.

Perhaps the gal is only slight—
    Could not have won my heart.
No sound, no image left of her—
    But marker, Maugham, and art.

Moonchild

IN all matters rational—

Until you start to quote the goddess,
Talk with spirits, build your charts ...

Tonight, when you pay homage to Hecate,
You might pray for sanity.

Fertility

A WEARY way it is, this strange desire.
I want to sleep, but for this fire—
The call of love in the chamber's bed
Filling up the bewildered head,
Until the hands grope in the dark,
Find the folded pages stark,
Find the pen there, barely clinging
(A muted light shows hands a-wringing),
And gently nudge the body's art,
Guide the bold and mindful dart,
Seek the rule of lines by night
(Always a bit off, for lack of sight).
I hope and pray for fair reception—
The goal is easily this conception—
Prized and pleasured of the lyre,
To bear the child of such strange desire.

Marginalia

I SEE it there, the riddle's care,
Buried midst those faded leaves,
Word upon its word, and lost,
Thought and spent and tucked away,
Fairing well, but oft hollow things—
Art, not they, but so in part—
Artful of their carelessness,
Fleeting spirits, age with age,
Desperate of their wormy graves.

Eugenis

THIS demand: Gods, take note of me!
Vain this line, I know, but what a vanity!

Too long have you slumbered on high,
Drinking of the vine, while earth falls dry.

What complaint is leveled, to what end—
Too many souls, perhaps, too vast to mend?

Then mend mine, I dare, O gods, mend mine,
And start with just a little wine.

It is yours to lift me above this earth;
So do so now, O mighty ones—*prove* your worth.

Many years of fear—it must defect
That who are left might stand again erect.

Assume your role, a conscience deep and large,
A charge of man, to keep man in charge.

Angrily I offer myself, if such must be,
So use my impertinence, my audacity.

What, some token to repel my doom?—
But to find some modern hecatomb!

No ox or sheep, I'm afraid—it's just not done.
These lines alone must do, let that be won.

Dispense with formality or ritualistic power,
Yes, I provoke with claims and claim this very hour.

Remember, this small figure was your own design.
Its intrepid heart is jealous; now give up what's mine!

By now this missive all the gods have heard;
Open your eyes, for heaven's stirred!

If not enough these words in your ears ring,
Then here's one man for stately halls to bring

Arrows, jagged, poised to prick the head;
So turn and feel a little sting in your supernal bed.

The gods may roll and crush the millions there,
But I'm a stubborn ant, prepared to bear

All that's hidden of Fate and saintly Muse,
And highest wisdom that noble man accrues.

Laugh, laugh, if you will, at this little buzz,
But I know all that will be is all that was—

Which is why all gods fail not to bend the knee.
Look up, O gods, and then take note of me!

Persona

"WHY write us?"—whence his rôle
    Upon my earthbound slate;
And something stirred within my soul
    That I could not articulate …

Never will—so there was pity in me,
    And I wrote him out, myself to sate,
Remembering days pondering upward:
    "Why create?"

Love Poem

YOU are a poem to me—
In fact, number 23.

If that offends you, understand:
Love is foremost in my hand,

Where by pen or keys conferred,
You become my written word.

The Library at Alexandria

NO thought can force a grimace
As one I have of tomes
Lost amidst destruction
Near Alexandrian homes.

No great amount of digging,
Or bibliopolic rite,
Or long-browed erudition
Will free what's recondite.

My only hope's in heaven,
Whence the past Callimachus calls;
As he, I'd choose eternity
In Alexandrian halls.

But I fear my chance of seeing
His fiery-fated books
Is bound forever after
In hateful, grimaced looks.

You see, to enter heaven
By pardon one must live,
But the men who burnt that hallowed place
Are men I can't forgive.

The Reader-King

OH, to read a book today,
To read a little book—
How I would lie,
    How I would die,
        Or *kill*
           To read a book.

Kill, and kill again, oh yes—
Just for the printed word,
And if it didn't satisfy
    (A prospect too absurd,

Unthinkable that one would dare
To botch the blissful book,
And were I crowned a reader-king,
    He'd get a nasty look,

No—more than a look,
    A damning glare
That gets the gallows greased,
A view to make a man think twice
    When his pregnant pen's released)—

But I digress (too much stress?),
Just like a well-paged book—
How I would lie,
    How I would die,
        Or *kill*
           To read a book.

Standing on a Pier, Near Syria, A.D. 175

Verissimus worried.
His deeds, even the smallest of them, cut their own swaths now,
    pushing ripple and wave well beyond mortality's shore.
But what of his words? With so few readers and fading acclaim,
    what world would find his text a light when his own gray
    candle had gone black?

He consoled himself:
It seemed a mere fortnight ago that everyone donned the flaming
    Rufinus like one of those upmarket robes from Sicily—
But *now* where is the man, so readily praised on the lips of old men
    (and loved on the hips of young women)?
All read him well—and read him out!

He smiled …
Let my words be deeds—if not mighty vessels, then tiny boats,
    manned by fearless captains boarding—port to port—reader,
    friend, and dreamer.
Better a few on many, than many on one, which soon rolls the
    proudly heeling ship.

Jeroboam's Dilemma

IF I could find a rhyme for "poem,"
My couplet would be better done.

Away

NO learning here today.
Soon out the lights and out the head,
And down, down, upon this bed
Of pine, where pen and paper lie—
Why this high monotony,
Crushing curiosity?
Not his plan to try to try
My earnest mind, just the wit,
To trip me up, if I am fit—

Had he warned me of today,
I might have stayed away.

For Avon Knox

DEAR CU   If you plan
To help with the decorations
For the formal at Indianapolis
Please meet in the Main Dorm Lobby
At 6:30 p.m. Thursday evening
And we will all go together
Wherever we are going
To work   Those of you
Who are coming on later
Can ask the girl at sign-out
Where we are and then
Come on over   Please
Be there for we need
Your help   Thanks
A lot   Trudy

Beaufort

THERE it is, progressiveness,
In that mighty country home
Where Painter and Prelate rendezvoused,
And Philosopher informed the Poet,
For the work of self-discovery and sublime.

Look, it is quite simple, she said,
Reason and rhyme, reason and rhyme ...

Poet's Resolution

I SHALL not use "Alas!" in poems,
Which makes me sound inane.
Nor shall I force the rhyme of words—
Alas! I've slipped again.

Odd

SO in touch with Nature were you,
In deference to an airy god
Up and up her sounds came to you,
Until the still grass whispered through you—
As I recall, you found "affinity" with sod—

Which is just a little odd.

A Peculiar Power

THIS period is of the head
And not of the heart
It is Intellectual rather than Emotional
Imitative rather than Creative
It is Prose written in rhyme
Lacks true poetic spirit
Lacks reference to nature too
From reading one might almost
Think the sun does not shine
Nor the birds sing
Nor the flowers grow

Dark

HOW he loved a tortured soul!—
(His own, of course) and played that rôle
For those who took sorrow in their art,
And revered the wounded heart.

He spoke of crying quite a lot,
And wrestled "forces," even fought
Angels, demons (troublesome beings ...
He could not *speak* of these things).

All murk and melancholy,
Futility and life-is-folly:
So deep and black his vacant stare,
Many perceived in him *despair.*

Yes, life is hard, but harder—hardest!—
For him who *feels* as feels the artist.
And thus his hope of joy is found
When joy is crushed and hope is bound.

(I, for one, spied a ruse—
And so, betwixt his tearful blues,
Suggested that he end it all
And thus uncloud my own dark soul ...)

Death of a Poet

SOMEONE said your death throes
Were like your poems,
Sad and violent and bitter.

Too bad your poems didn't matter.

Class Reunion

CURIOUS that we want to rediscover
The many faces lost to time's resolve.
All have felt the spurn of fickle youth,
Which dallies off in some nostalgic land.
Every knee now disregards the King and Queen,
For it cannot bend without a bit of stress;
Every head has lost its crown or glory,
Every eye its sheen;
Bodies either plumped or undernourished,
Skin in fall's frame withered away;
And chins, once strong and hopeful,
Despite the buoyancy of happy surprise,
Mime the assembly's gravity and decay.

Kings of Youth

A JOY to listen to aging's caterwaul—

Those of us who missed splendor's reign:
Life so sweetly crashes all!

We revel in our heads
As they take to their peasanted beds:

We stay somewhat the same ...

They fall.

Bad Age

A BAD age for wanderers,
    For readers, for ponderers;
A bad age for dreamers,
    For poets, for schemers;
A bad age for tinkerers,
    For triflers, for thinkerers—

You see? A bad age for
    thinkerers ...

The Clouds, the Wind

WHENCE cometh the murky clouds?
Perhaps from Pamela's head.
And the vaunting, lordly wind?
Her husband, Ed.

Idler's Year

I KEEP dreaming I will one day get off this couch,
And turn off that damnable television and trash the remote,
And maybe, just maybe, do something important
With my pathetic life. But then I get the urge
To make ramen noodles or a frozen pizza;
I do, and I eat until I'm sick
And have to sit down again.

The whole year has gone by this way.
The next one promises no better day.

Up All Night

Up all night, a worthy goal—
How I had planned to spend it well!
But I squandered my lonesome hours
For lack of focus, like a drunken man—
Body, awakened; sense, asleep:
I should have worked on dreams instead.

Current

LETHARGY!—so goes the leaf
Whose winds cannot stir.
Its season is its grief—
Barely fall, soon winter

(Spring's forgot, and summer, a song
Unsung)—the pale folio
Lies at rest too long;
And the stem below

Has no impetus to etch
Its fossil print (save
This diminutive batch)
To an immortal grave.

How flat it lies, now flatter still,
And feels no weight of occasional shoe,
But only wearisome will,
And waits for snow;

It scant'ly breathes what life is left,
Remembers spring's soon reborn,
And hopes against hope bereft,
That moldy coats are shorn.

But then, the fear (lethargy's sire)—
That spring's sprung too soon for me,

And I, my work undone, retire
To obscure eternity.

Such a fate may be enough
To conjure up some ancient draft
That rankles this dormant stuff,
Liberating art and craft.

Might I find a current, an ageless sheer,
That carries echoes thence
Of leaves that would deny the year
Despite their circumstance?

Oh, to lift the head!
To refuse this earthly bed!

Liberty Dollars

WHAT compels me to make more of it
    Is not the stuff,
For which I am so often their slave;
    I have enough,
But to be freed from *them*—
    That I crave.

Cat Lies All Day

CAT lies all day on a pillow in the sun,

Then yawns and stretches and pads away,

Until it reaches another room,

And finds a new pillow and spends the night.

Judgment

DEPART from me, ye accursed, into everlasting futility,
Prepared for deadbeats, loafers and dreamers,
Who spend years thinking about doing, but never do.
Behold, thy rudderless ship!

In Absentia

AGAIN! something I didn't know, now do,
And will forget within a day or two.

The Phantom

I ACCOSTED him in a sort of dream,
And asked in tears if he recalled my name.
"As it was," he said, "as it soon will be"—
And departed with no farewell.

I awoke, or found myself alone,
My arm outstretched and grasping the air.
No more the man to grace my tiny realm,
No more shared the beating heart.

Scent

I REMEMBER that you died
When for the day I've spent
The charge of all your living,
Which came and back was sent.

And even at dark your being
Shines bright as was your face,
Far, but from a promised shore
Of your so-called resting place.

I sleep, then finally sleep,
And just as the eyes go out,
I catch your scent upon my pillow
And lose the last of doubt.

The Willful Child

OUT there, somewhere, beneath the crashing waves,
Young Abhimanyu, feeling quite at home, stayed on—

Amma, down to four from nine, could search no more
And let the sea rage through her frantic eyes,
Condemning thousands in a wave of grief.

When the torrent broke, she sang, "Aiee!
No company for your brothers are you, my little Abhu,
For they sleep in fetid graves, while you
    frolic in the sea."

Out there, somewhere, beneath the waves,
No love returns but memory.

White House

IF one can step into a demon's lair,
You felt it there in that white, tormented house,
Sensed some dark master looming,
Antiquely jointed, toed and notched,
Sealed in a paisley skin,
And watching, with warped-windowed eyes.

It was no surprise to you, this bivouac,
And there the family anxiously paused
As you contemplated your fate.
Such were the times, when evil powers
Rationed America's heart for fuel,
And rendered the dream a fool's ambition.

The house's acquisition was the soul itself;
Its foul spirit had its way with you,
Throwing fire and ice, loss and death,
And countless prickly things your way,
Until you were on your knees in tears,
Crying, "Accursed, accursed …"

Ulisse

THE sons left one by one,
    And there you were, my father,
Wandering in that vast and barren sea
    Beyond Troy's embattled walls.
The war was still raging in your mind,
    And neither Penelope's faithful arms
Nor remembrance of Calypso's love
    Could calm your furious soul.
How did pitiless mortality wrench it all
    From your metal-worn hands?
How surprised we were to find empty
    Your rough-hewn throne ...

Watch for us, my father. The sons
    Have not forgotten your Ithaca.

Success

BEFORE my father died, he asked
To be buried in jeans and a tee-shirt,
Laid out in a plain, unfinished box.
By this, he claimed, snubbing the world,
He would be defining success.

I still believe he was right, but
We put him in a suit for the rest.

Ghosts of Greenlawn

I SEE those stones daily,
Dim reminders of lives lost to time's relentless machinations;
Yet noble testaments to greater glory than mere clammy earth,
Buried in it, but pointing upward to meet the glowing sky;
Straight as soldiers, and some as if fallen,
And even then their words boldly declaring, not death,
But existence itself—what was, yet is …

I see those stones in a highway's glance,
And pass without emotion, pondering none of its kind—
No stirrings of ancient lives in me, but mine alone,
The soul that is here and now, so unlike their own.
They are a corner's vision of the unstoppable ahead,
And press themselves upon a mind already full
Of today's miniscule but insistent tasks,
And dare ask, inaudibly, that I not forget …

I see those stones arise—arise—
But barely glimpse the men and women, children, in marbled history:
Ghosts of Greenlawn beckon me!
All these years and only from a distance have I wandered there;
Only in my mind have my fingers touched their chiseled faces,
Dour, bright, sad and light, all noting this truth,
That they are home and I am not—a traveler bound
From place to place, plot to plot,
Until my own small marker

Bids me stop.

The Disease

YOU sold your herbal wares
    To every frail disciple—
Transfused hope for blood—
    Swapped word for bread.

You told them, "Reject the pain,"
    And claim their "eternal now,"
So that all who stayed believed—
    Beyond reason, believed—

Until one day you seemed
    Abruptly old——
And the next day your parts
    Shut themselves off.

Shaker

MOTHER Ann,
I thank thee
For killing off your crank design
In liege to celibacy—
Thus women throw off restrictive twine,
Immortal'ing men by lycium vine,
Who revel in what seems more divine,
And thank thee.

Tabloid

"LOOK here," she smartly read,
'Man sires love-child at 84!' "
"So *he* was told," said a friend
Who knew the score.

Cruel Banquet

WANT it all; permitted none.
    What sort of spread is this
That wets the tongue
    And denies the kiss?

Run, the Raw Hail

SHE hurls the stones that crush the soul;
Invites the storm and devours it whole;
Commands black columns to rain insult,
Frees vile serpents to root out fault;
Clutches rank poisons in her bottomless purse—
Compact and chaos, hairbrush and curse;
Steals with great cruelty the things you control;
She hurls the stones that crush the soul.

Whispered Words

I REMEMBER your anguished threat:
"If you leave me, I'll kill myself."
I stayed, and so kept you alive,
And you repaid me by making life hell.
Now you lie hooked to machines,
Hovering between life and death,
And I'm telling you now,
This time for real,
I'm leaving …

Purpose

WHAT is the point of my life?
Today I will answer:

    To please,
      To placate,
        To put up with

    Women.

Kiss

Is it right to be thinking of that perennial kiss
When task and tether prod us ever forward?
A mere moment!—then years gone, and time amiss,
And still there, those of whom we are solely steward.
Not right, I'd say, and you'd say it, too,
But for those flashes, like sudden wafts
Of lilac or rose, that make us either rue
What went on before, or love, or laugh.
If a good day (or bad), we spend it wandering,
Far too long at the behest of a fleeting spring,
Leaving routine to others—say, sweeping or laundering—
That we may let memory in, and let it sing.
For, sooner or later those cells will die,
And there will be no kiss, nor you, nor I.

Dress Up

CALL me
what you will,
but
I think this
world's a better place
when a woman's in a dre
ss.

Bitter Waters Lay Below

I

SWEET love is no conqueror of lands, that's true,
And also true, that once I thought it so—
I have learned a little, you know!
Such is the best of growing old
And if done gracefully, I just might recall
Everything that's good, and let all else go.

II

She was no land, no kingdom to rule,
Again how true—pardon my unkind figure;
Yet how hard not to king her!
A people within one person, all bundled up,
A lost flock, or, at the least, one sheep for many,
And I, with a shepherd's heart to bring her.

III

I loved her—how I loved!—we loved as one
More than much, each glorious pairing
A blissful act of daring—
On my part alone (still conqueror then,
Remember, land), for mine was restoration,
And you a prospect, sharing.

IV

And yet, despite my complete surrender,
Daily making your face adoration's aim,

I saw nothing of the same,
Not in your melancholy eyes, or fleeting smile,
No real love, but more an act of taking,
A sure path to sorrow and shame.

V

As your baseless tears carved tell-tale routes
Upon a face that struggled to ever blue,
We as young lovers were through.
The pout, the whine, the cry—still sweet,
Yes, but tainted by my revelation from within:
You were no land, that much I knew.

VI

Bitter waters lay below the woman there;
And no sweet words would save that rootless heart—
How our love once seemed art!—
Now broken land itself, nothing to conquer,
Except that undefined dearth, a desert,
And all of why we had to part.

The Hummingbirds

THERE has not been a month, a week, a day,
in which we did not span
this cold, gray gulf,
and try to have our way,
risking all above unforgiving waters—
like migrating birds above the waters,
loving, loving o'er the waters—
Until the call
from shore ...

I might account the hours as our own—
but life decrees we stay apart,
and holds not love in high esteem,
deriding these flutters and waves of passion
that lift our souls among the flowers,
hummingbirds among the flowers,
loving, loving o'er the flowers—
Until the call
from shore ...

Confession

I HAVE failed you, Lord, again. The body is
A den of thieves, the soul itself a harlot.

Out

WHAT of this fire?
I cannot love unless coals burn bright;
Or breathe if not put out tonight.

Grail

DID I find a mournful shade retreating beyond the pane,
Or was it some odd trick of light, or the tears of nature's rain?
'Twas you, I think, with more repose than I would ever share—
You, reflecting illicitly from out its glassy stare.
    Did I find a shade, my love, and was that shade your own?
    (Were your thoughts with me, my love, e'en as I wandered home?)

Did I find a pensive form just past a sacred field,
Your dangerous hair a little mussed by wind, and age revealed?
'Twas you, I think, though distance made for doubtful summer skies—
You, though melancholy may have clouded up my eyes.
    Did I find a form, my love, and was that form your own?
    (Were your thoughts with me, my love, e'en as I wandered home?)

Did I find an impassioned one still searching for the grail,
Or was it just a wild strand upon our errant trail?
'Twas you, I think, obsessed, but staid, about our lives unplanned—
You, subdued, but mindful of the embers in your hand.
    Did I find the one, my love, and is this one your own?
    (Were your thoughts with me, my love, e'en as I wandered home?)

Petals

SHE loves me—
> But I have plucked those years away,
> Hoping love would have its day …

She loves me not—
> Dream-hued petals on the floor,
> The last to fall …
>> She loves me not!
>>> She—loves—me—*not!*
>> How revelation seeks to rot
>>> All that's come before …

Epiphany

I SHOULD have known!
Sweet words hide a ghastly tone.
Murmurs feed a deeper moan.
Man won't calm the spirit's groan,
For earthly love is earth's alone.

The Shaman

SHE looked away at this his darkest hour, and found another,
And in those dreams of youth and passion, woke again to
     life inside her,
Found the swan again inside her, felt his breath upon her fire,
Blowing, blowing, breathing, blowing, gently on her glowing embers,
Till the flames of self consumed her, till the first was gone.

The first he sat in ravaged silence, helpless as an aging native,
Desperate for her adoration, feeling adoration slipping,
Felt the path before him slipping, crumbling o'er the dark abyss—
The hopeless crawl above the canyon, as love itself decides to fail,
Every movement soft considered, the black alone,
     above the waters ...

She could not love admit renewed for him the young,
     the saving savage;
And love believed?—that golden fruit had perished with the
     years of longing.
Orphic chants and mystic powders mesmerized her wonder still,
But ah, the younger!—her wilding pagan, his lovely eyes,
     his burning lips;
He held the firebrand and stirred her, stirred the
     love denied within ...

The old one drifted, closing his eyes, floating o'er the
     boundless chasm,
Wondered would the old spells hold him, stop the jaws'
     voracious closing?

Rhythmic worlds had dissipated; earth's vocations he failed and
      failed him;
Friends had fled; and families vanquished; faith was razed; and
      fire diminished—
Fool! to think that incantation's hope could hold her till the end!

And so it goes, in love, with love, which dies, discards and
      finds anew.
The Shaman's fusty art was true, but now, in her heart, antiquity.
Love as smoke and flash by night, soon distant as the icy stars,
Cannot compete with kiss caress and promises of bodied warmth,
And visions of the burning ring, of carnal love
      between her thighs.

The song the curse the prayer the spell the chant the rite the
      poem—in vain!
The elder wept, reduced to ashes, deeply o'er the
      dark winds blowing,
Dangling there he watched her glowing, watched his
      ancient lover glowing,
Felt the other's savage breathing, blowing youth into her heart,
Whisper'ing love beyond horizons, stoking strength to
      sear his heart.

Pause

WHEN freed from dreams, impure or sweet,
And rising from your lonesome bed
    to stalwart-stand upon your feet,
Pause, my love, the good morning greet—
        and say my name.

Cared and carried into our town,
Among the many thousands there,
    the men and women loveless-bound,
Forget not that you have loved, and love was found—
        and say my name.

The stone is heavy, the waters swift;
How soon our love had overflowed
    and threw love down—and now, bereft,
Please think of me—this one small gift—
        and say my name.

Before or past the wanton chore
(Perhaps I've fled—or not, perhaps,
    and thought to lock the damning door)
I give you pause, to see me there, as before,
        and say my name.

At close when lingering dots the night,
My lips still part in those memories,
   and kiss your eyes' fair-fawning light;
How dare, in starry flashes, these thoughts indite,
   that in your heart should flourish fame—
   and pause to ponder passion's claim—
      and say my name.

Goodbye

GOODBYE, friend.
I'm afraid this is goodbye.
With me it's never see ya later,
Or *ciao*, or *cayacama*;
Never till we meet again,
Hasta la vista or *dewa mata*;
Surely not *auf Wiedersehen*,
Or sunny *sizobonana*.
Aloha, yes, it may be so,
But don't expect again hello.

You are loved, so don't be sour,
For it fits the time no longer.
The chapter's finished,
The page is turned,
The wave is given,
At last, it's done—

Goodbye.

Last Day

SO many mid to all night visits here.
I know these walls too well and know them dark,
The shadowed desks, the low-lit aisles,
The window's garland of city lights—

Ah, to walk away! To spend alone
This final day in obscurity, to let
History slip, however slight, with
Muted friends who cannot say farewell.

The Heron

OUT of place so near to me it seems,
But not by this quiet pond,
    Not now, before dawn—
    The mind above is plainly drawn …

At the water's edge so still,
I race to catch the tall, blue heron—
    From the mound a statuette—
    Wondrous beauty in silhouette.

You're here—I sense it—but then,
More near, the heron swifts away—
    Suddenly, the cold … but not without
    The good that kills doubt.

Home But Not

AFTER three days of enduring wood and smoke
    I showered,
And washed away all things identifiable
Only by God and forensics.

Many things fell away;
    But neither nature nor civilization
Revealed dignity
Or made me feel at home.

The End

I DIDN'T see the clouds roll in,
But saw the air in somber yellows, pinks;
Watched the shadows slink beneath the tiles;

Wondered as the waters on the stove
Refused to boil; watched as little children
Lost their play and stopped;

Heard the silence of the birds, run aground;
Felt the weight of heaven by rippled cloud,
A fine, antique ceiling, ready to collapse.

"The end?" a neighbor asked of my sinking heart,
But he seemed to be only mouthing words,
Which would not carry for lack of wind.

Spirit

SHE sensed, she said, the soul of an ancient lover,
Long dead, drifting like fumes among walls and rafters,
    Playful like a dust,
And settling at the foot of her vacuous bed.

I marveled—perhaps aloud—at her calm demeanor:
Was she not afraid? I asked (as I trembled more than a little).
Was she not full of wonder and joy, as anyone should imagine?
    No, twice, *no*—then a third time this:

Did she not long for solid arms than a wisp,
Warm, real flesh than disembodied skin,
A sonorous voice than romantic wind,
    And lips?

This time no reply—and so I saw in modern man
The death of fear and awe and love—and took my leave
To search soul after dripping soul, to each concluding,
    Thou dost not believe!

To a Future Reader

IF we end in the cesspit of barbarity,
And find we must rebuild from the ground up,
Forced to scratch our way back to humanity,
Crawling long after walking and running too far,
And then centuries later, take a new step
Toward understanding,

I pray, O curious one, you will let them know
I saw it coming.

Evolution

HOW like an ape, by naked arm and leg;
How like a snail, by sluggish contrition;
How like a king, by enterprise and carriage;
How like an angel, by unearned position.

Surely proof—though less than science—
    Of evolution's trail.
To one or more of these I'm bound,
But where to look, up or down?

Faith

SOME say it's easy; I say, not so—
Oh, for half the little seed they claim to sow!

Belief is simple, to that I concede—
Just point by point, with proofs long decreed.

But faith—living it—now, that's something more:
I'm to be all of Eden after it's closed the door!

Yes, I knocked, and it was opened, and I stepped in—
But how easy to walk right out again.

Oh, to be the new man, and on to the sky!
But the old one's a specter, refusing to die.

Any wonder I struggle at what little I've got?
Any wonder I *strain* to be what I'm not?

Master Time

TIME—cruel monarch—why command a fool as I to travel
Every misty track once laid and now secured by devil?
How often must I trace the steps that I decline to follow?
Pitiless Time, by mirrored fate, have mercy lest I wallow!
    (Pitiless, yes, and loveless folly,
    Where smile is fuel for melancholy.)

Time, release me from your corridors so long and grim,
Whose abysmal, backward stretches are the dark descent from dim,
And on those walls your photographs of haunted, captured souls—
Sharp-eyed Time, why preserve what every moment kills?
    (Sharp, this pain and abiding folly,
    Where smile is fuel for melancholy.)

Master Time, what promise do you offer from my birth?
Indeed! It is mine to thank you for this hollow march of death?
I thank not you, but only He whose favors all must crave,
Who offers liberty to one who cowers here as slave.
    (Beyond is hope from eternal folly,
    Where smile is fuel for melancholy.)

Time—dark master—when will I be free from every instance,
Bundled cruelly, with all that's bad or good, in reminiscence?
I pray for life well-lived, indeed, but also life again;
Vanquished, Time, to make a moment now, and never then—
    (Vanquished, yes, and so this folly,
    Where smile is fuel for melancholy.)

Sunset

WOULD this fire-palette stir me so
Were I to anticipate,
Not the morning's finished work,
But a crashing canvas at the Painter's command?

All There Is

IF this is all there is, my friend,
And life's a breath, a puff of smoke,
Our dreams just dreams within a dream,
Our plans a pointless itinerary—

As oft I've heard your lips confess—

Will you protest when I have your possessions,
That house on the beach, those glorious cars,
Your beautiful wife, whom I covet still—
In short, your life, your will?

Upon what code will your objections rest?

A Darkened Dream

THE house no longer holds the vision;
It cannot contain its formative lines.

The rooms, the lights—
Is everything dead?
The endless shelves of well-thumbed books ...

The swirl of heat and scent ...

Here in these veins guests wandered;
Now only shadows, dusty and long—
Admirers, dreamers, lovers—
Gone!

Wall, hearth, mantle—old as old,
Each forgetting others in the struggle,
Now of termite and black mold.

Ah, in flashes, I do remember ...
But fragile memory, can it save you?

Time restructures thought and space—
How less I know what I once knew!

How small the house, how soon repacked,
Its walls bowing in a desperate check,
Its nooks filled, its paths a-strewn

With contraband and errant buys—

All is fraught with bulky things,
Rusted, in ruin, marked by neglect,
Vying for space in too modest a space ...

I have sat too long.

I should not have closed my eyes.

I should not have dared to dream—

I saw the castle crumbling there,
The market sold, the curtains torn,
The courtyard emptied of lovers' song,
The windows revealing only years—

I filled its moat with tears ...

I slept for days, ignoring the sun:
I could not be stirred by the hand of earth;
Could not be moved to build again;
Could not be revived by impassioned skies ...

And when the call had finally come,
Up! Awaken! Dream again—

Night had filled my eyes.

Companion

DOG, come rest beside me,
And console a weary man.
The autumn day is over,
The time of dreams at hand.

Dog, come rest beside me,
And guard against the night.
I think I may have need again
Your sense of black and white.

Rest beside me, lonely friend,
And wile the time away.
Together let us quietly
Close another day.

Darwin Rediscovered

SO are ya tellin' me that if I was t'strip
The sorry ol' skin off Charlie's head,
And bury it beneath a cliff,
I cou'n't feed a believer a little
Un-natural see-lection?
Have ya seen that ol' boy's head?
Have ya seen that monkey's ledge?

To Pain

HOW my pain loves me so!
Up to greet me upon each dreamlike dawn;
Lies in wait—in state—as I trudge off to bed;
And all the moments ticking in between
Punctuate each deftly plotted aggravation,
The dull, the sharp, the worrisome and alarming:
Relentless lover, release me from these bonds …

The damaged, earthen body,
Once made for heaven's pristine cordiality,
Is turned away by the curse of isolation,
And remembers this in each isolating act,
Every little spot of the fallen's grief,
Tiny pinpricks to remind and to enlighten
The common man that common he is not!

Many have forgotten—that is very true—
And the most insensible man will refuse to hear
Dear pain calling the world to attention,
Holding on sharply to earth's reverie;
But were this man to die and fly to the perfect place,
Oh, how that former life would likely seem,
Evaluating to a torture, to a disfiguring dream.

But man rejects such a series of exclamations,
For pain—that ruthless lover—hides well beneath the sheets,
Coursing through the veins most subtly,

Content to tap, tap, tap him on the shoulder,
Or, when really angered, kick him in the back!
This attack begins at birth and contemplates the grave,
Where it must die as its assailant leaps away.

Today my pain is with me and seeks caresses,
And I am complicit in this lengthy arrangement;
Though secretly I think to enlist the help of priests,
Who, in selling me a pill or machine or method,
Claim that they can exorcise the fiend, and bring
The whole of bliss to me now—sending her away …
But to whom, I wonder, to love what wanton lover?

No, I will keep her, for she is mine alone;
I know her face and form and peculiarities.
She's interlaced among my ravished, dying cells,
And loves each joint and promises worse for wear,
Promises to hold me close until the very end,
My heartbeat skipping with every breath
That struggles by passion against the smell of death.

Cancer

TOO little time and too much of it wasted.
A slug has more purpose than I tonight;
It grimes along to get from here to there,
Defiance in its slow and silent crawl.

Mike, your personal war instructs us daily
To never throw a moment away—
So intimate you are with fear and trembling
For what we can only pretend is coming.

Act of God

STAY, old man, and die—
Not my place to hold you back—
So determined for your rough demise
Upon a storm: I realize
I cannot change your morbid track.

We both "seek higher ground"—your cry—
But mine's quite dry; yours, a bloody bath;
And I suppose my years unspent leads me;
Yours emptied—no longer needs me,
But somehow "needs" its wrath …

The Soccer Field

I'D rather see the empty field in the early morn—

    The low-lying fog lifting the dewy terrain,
    As if to release its prior bout in a sweat,
    Struggle and chaos crystallizing their domain,
    And raising a promise, warmed for a brand-new day,
    Of victory-for-all upon this battered plain—

Than in the evening, after all have gone home,
    Half in rapture, half overcome.

Arrogance

A WINDY buzz, and a little laugh at that,
Then paused too long upon a wall—
He was a fly, after all …
But Sam was a fly-eating cat.

Forgotten

HOW wretched a life for its days of toil
Beneath the damning sun! No soul
Remembered when your time was done,
And so, like a crow upon the sea,
Flapped and floundered until you fell
Beneath the waves. Not even your own
Heard your final cries as you made your peace,
And now your children, strewn like flotsam,
Know only that some ol' rotten drunk
Shot a friend; and neither you nor friend,
For mama's sake, was ever seen again.

Mutable

I have swooned beneath the crisp, winter sky,
And let it draw my spirit high.

Other times, in that same brittle air,
I have known unfathomable despair.

Either I or sky is mutable in this matter.
For my part, I suggest the latter.

Broken Things

WE cannot fully answer why—
Except to say, in the name of freedom, something went awry—

And only hope that in the end the Maker has in mind
The fix of broken things as part of his design …

Life is a Haunt

LIFE is a haunt,
A hope that disobeys,
A cry that wants of endings—
Of fear, a dampened store—
Dim through, the faded candle:
Open the door!

Trouble Brewing

A CRYSTAL night,
Stars for a change more bright
Than the torch-lit streets below.
Surely they abhor the sight.

Reparation

MONEY'S rumored a filthy thing,
Passed hand-to-hand from rich to poor and back again,
Kicked about through a muddied land.

It is of use as a reciprocal measure,
Of goods, of trade—nothing more—
Certainly not of humanity's store.

Refuse it!—it lacks that dignity
That you have won by fearful days.
It cannot assuage what pride alone allays.

Money's for the here and now, and thus,
Beneath us all to surrender or to chase
For sins well left to history's trace.

Like peoples untold, you stood to count,
And so you count, and more for *want* of compensation.
Let it go!—partake in the greatest reparation—

Purchased in blood, this humanity,
Wrested from the hands of some who named it,
But morally never claimed it.

September 11

REGAL cloud and somber sky, like gods, remain
Downcast searchers of the space below,
Where two towers, united by freedom's reign,
Testament to triumph, bane to iniquitous foe,
Once proudly stood. Therein yet cling
Heroic spirits braving hell for the stranger's cry,
Heartless fate against them; above, on stolen wing
Iblis and his craven demons fly;
Below the fallen reprise their tragic rôle,
Staged without end for a grief-stricken nation,
Whose liberty, imposing itself upon the soul,
Rejects America's defeat or abdication.
Thus, this haunted ground reveals a silhouette,
Two towers standing tall lest men forget.

History Left Unsung

HISTORY left unsung will leave
To harsher tones the present day;
Finds the doomist in grand, dark strokes;
Lets defeatists have their way.

War and war, and whispers of war,
Disturb provincial ears,
Deaf to horrors, cries and pain,
For ignorance of boundless years.

History, left unsung, is pleased
When page and eye no longer greet;
For by that way the lesson's learnt,
And kills the chance repeat.

The Fighters

It is a country's muted cry that lies there deep within
The secret pain of mothers, who in blackest grief must bear
What their sons' and daughters' land as a light is compelled to share
With all the world. We see, but feel not what the brave have felt,
The call for sacrifice of freedom this very freedom to defend,
The giving of life and love that hope is born again,
And reason enough for the fallen men a hand so sorely dealt.

The fighters scramble upon a word born of wind and rage,
Fire and sand, death and dirge, to repel man's desperation;
What liberty has reared, has again reared its head, this nation
Bent not on conquest, but willing to conquer those evil men
Who stand against the good and free, and seek to end this age,
Raising themselves as gods; thereupon this war to wage
Without regard to where or when, against the errant heart of man.

Say what you will of peace and love, and cravenly whine!
But make no mistake, this love will sometimes kill, and kill it must;
It opens hell's jaws for the wicked, and expedites heaven for the just.
For goodness' sake the storm arrives upon the blighted shore,
And peace is happy in patience to wait to meet up with the divine;
It knows that some must die to stop the land's decline,
And dune must crumble and rise again to end what all abhor.

Peace, yes—but for now the locusts seek to devour
The fields of innocents who inhabit this ancient rock.
The dutiful river carries on and without an earthly clock

Attempts to stop erosion as the sand turns into mud;
It wanders, slowly, silently, around a lonely tower,
And reminisces of an ageless garden, and waits for the better hour,
When its banks no more ask of it the siphoning of blood.

Those will be our happy times, all others merely endured,
A long, long road whose heavy toll seemed oft too great a cost;
And then the mothers of darker days will find their loved and lost,
Kings and queens who rule the land these storms would help renew,
And with them, us, in gratitude, and liberty secured.
So speaks the rock, remember!—let no name be obscured.
For the weak are ever with us, and heroes always few.

I pause—I must—despite the comings and goings, weeks and days;
I pause to wonder at men who surrender all for the grand ideal,
Fathers, sons, and sons of sons, whose faces will reveal
The hope that dwells within this land, and in the land to be,
And defend this place—while I stay home, in a sort of cozy haze
Of self-indulgent leisure, wherein I soon neglect to praise
The fighters who leave these open shores to give their lives for me.

Somme

TWENTY thousand, sealed on that terrible day,
Found themselves knocking at heaven's gate.
"It begins," muttered a long-time resident saint,
Watching the recruits in resigned dismay;

And seeing none whom on earth he held dear,
Returned to his work and bowed his head;
Until another saintly creature said,
"A million souls within the year

May find our lustrous cloud crashing in
By weight of men and blood-soaked ground!"
And so they regarded the swelling sound,
Which seemed a mixture of gunfire and sin.

Days of Despair

DAYS of despair have come,
When all things hopeless kill the spirit,
And demons surround the house and heart.

Where the hosts to defend us?
Where the thunder and brandished sword?
Nothing left but earth and ash, O Lord.

Emptiness and heartache drown the soul,
And into the fire the body seared;
How long abide these faithless tears?

From the abyss the spirit shrieks,
From the knee I cry out, "I do believe;
Lord, help my unbelief!"

Exile

HOW came I suddenly to this place?
My way impeded by trunk and trim, as it were, a forest,
Primitive, raw, sickly, dark—rank with leafy mold
Sloughed at seasons' hearts' command and lying amidst
The damp and listless remains of a life that I once knew.
Yet here, in this misted land, where sun declines to penetrate
And sight declines to see—here the eyes burn like fire
For want of those tears that have poured upon the ground,
Demanding their own way, reckless in their abandonment,
Eager to form rivulets that seek a brighter path
And scatter to the left and to the right, as if they too
Can bear me no more.

As shadow prays to night, the very dropping of my lids
Remembers my hours of sorrow upon this rotted floor;
But my own petitions can neither tower nor top
The hundreds around me who have already found their light.
The heart is sick; the head, heavy; the hand, empty ...
For want of my Heaven on earth, I cannot find heaven!
Were I to even glimpse again that Evening Star,
Her face no longer beckons, nor light seems near:
Her very nearness proves the vastness between us,
Pleading, No more! deserving no more of my holy light
You are for loving cruelly and taking cruel love—
And thus, my ghostly form ...

II

Now kneeling, now standing, and just as sudden,
My clammy soul is parched by fire, feels
The callous sands about me, the savage sun,
In ruthless affection, sears the scalp's stragglers,
And deeper still, beyond my naked head,
Ignites remembrance—for what?—for torture!
And here, where tears dare not flow, they flow!
Hot as violence they level mirage and dune alike,
And blur the path before me, calling, taunting,
Wanderer! go here, go there, go forward, go back!
Ah, my friend, my love—soul of my soul!
Is there nothing left but desolation?

Each minute spans the desert itself, each step is endless—
But then, a market, where I may drift among the sellers,
Who, seeing the sign, recoil from my haggard form.
Yes, they recoil, men who have spurned the dark shadow;
Men who hide beneath awnings, preferring promise and dream,
Their buyers—the lovers—quickly blinded by sparkles,
Artless as flames that boldly flicker against the storm,
Deaf to the shrieking rocks that house the prophet,
Ignorant of the forlorn paramours who hide in the shadows ...
Nor will they be informed by me, a wind searching for a wind,
Who once explored the whole world in his lover's song,
But now knows only banal hellos.

III

My room is a prison of letters and books,
Where I find my story told and retold countless times.
I lie down and sleep, but I cannot sleep; my evil dreams
Force me to the side of my bed, my muscles taut,
My skin pulled like a shroud over broken bones,
My wild eyes searching but for a glimmer …
I should tear down these walls, open my windows,
But how my sinful soul finds pleasure in darkness!
How it insists upon memory's own fading gleam,
Which, in waking, seems like night, and in night, a terror!
O Sorrow, there is nothing left for you here …
Dear God, let her feed upon another!

How came I suddenly to this place?
My day's work is to get out of bed, my task to simply rise:
And I do, and go about business, and greet friend and guest;
But there you are, Belinda, ever centered among them,
As lovely as a flower, as carefree as jewelry,
Woman, mistress, mother, friend—I loved them all,
And love them still, each petal the fullness of my wonder,
Each facet perfect and brilliant and shining in you:
In you that glimmer … ah, but in that glimmer, exile,
With ample time to wonder how love was not enough—
Oh, my Love, what went wrong? O Love!
The heart, the heart, the heart!

The Dampened Spirit

THE rain began to seep within
The very layers of my skin,
Boring holes within my heart,
Tearing it apart.

But out the window, Anna's there!
Lets torrents gaily wash her hair.

Surely my dark mood is sin.

The Promise

BE it prison
   Of man,
   Or body,
   Or earth,
   I swear
   To you
   By God,
   I will break
   Free.

Little Page

LITTLE Page is a wind on wheels,
A roadrunner on her feet,
And when she thinks to swing,
Well, God help the swing.

Snow

If I were God (thank Him I'm not)
I would love mankind and guide his ways,
And let my nature fill his days,
And help him though he's forgot.

But just so often—no, regularly—
I'd look upon those ways and snort,
And out a powder, my sharp retort
Divine—thus beauteously

Blanket his house and fêted streets—
A silvery, crystalline spray
That lightens his night and darkens his day—
In cold and desolate sheets.

Man's walk would be slowed by this, you see;
He'd slip and sometimes genuflect,
And for a season be less erect,
And recall Me (that is, God, not me).

Sense of Justice

PEOPLE lament God's cruelty for
   Turning away all ignorance,
And rightly sense it can't be right,
   But never ponder the root of sense:

If God is just, as be he must,
   Then why not *trust* his recompense?

When Toughs Collide

BIG ol' John loomed above,
Wielding weight and a frequent shove,
Till I—reason or cowardice come—
Thought to give up pride and run;

Then wiry Ernie, from air it seemed,
Appeared—and John a coward deemed
In daring him to a different track—
And pushed the menace back.

Ah, how quickly a street-tough is "friend"—
Then back to the street, for there was the end
Of Ernie's love, who, the following day,
Told me to get the hell away.

I did, but first, upon my knees,
Prayed for Ernie—and for no reprise—
Lest again, when toughs collide,
I'll need a friend to save my hide.

The Fact

IF Stephen Jay Gould was wrong,
    He knows it full well right now.
If he was right, he knows

                Nothing.

There's This

I HAVE loved God all my life;

Yet

    Haven't felt him fill me up,
    Haven't heard his whispered word,
    Haven't seen the fabled cup,
    Haven't spoken Babel-speak,
    Haven't slipped the wrested thigh,
    Haven't been surprised by joy,
    Haven't been to Sinai.

Might I be tramping through darkened tombs
Like rebels or Semitic heretics?
Might I be wandering, sockets dry,
My ears waxed shut, my fingers clipped?

I have no miracles to watch unfold,
I have none, not one, no wine, no seas;
All's testimony and common sense,
All's evidence and humbled knees.

There's this (not much, but often enough;
And perhaps out there is one like me,

Whose grasp on harder things is weak,
But sees the proof in hand or tree):

> *From inside out the self is sensed,*
> *From one to others life's enhanced,*
> *From flesh entangled spirits wed,*
> *From tiny seeds souls are bred!*

I wait, but rarely watch the sky;
Remember creation's root's *create*,
Mimic in words this attribute,
And love, however reprobate;
Easy to sense that love is God,
So try, despite the world's dark strife,
Until the tomb, where I'm sure to say,

I have loved God all my life.

The Pleiades

YOUNG sisters, wrapped in ghostly nebulae,
Weep not that Science uncovers your secret parts.
Today's stargazers lift the veil brazenly,
But love every particle of your light,
And poets yet look upon your beauty,
Knowing no untoward advance at night,
Can stop your nymphal dance.

The Dream

By this quiet lake, do I not know God?
By forbidding forest, do I not know God?
    Not enough, it would seem,
    For *more* is the dream …

By man's great towers, do I not know God?
By speed of progress, do I not know God?
    Not enough, it would seem,
    For *more* is the dream …

By brother in battle, do I not know God?
In the season of sorrow, do I not know God?
    Not enough, it would seem,
    For *more* is the dream …

In the arms of my mother, do I not know God?
For the nod of my father, do I not know God?
    Not enough, it would seem,
    For *more* is the dream …

For the love of Belinda, do I not know God?
Just to whisper "Belinda," do I not know God?
    Not enough, it would seem,
    For *more* is the dream …

    And so, the Theme,
    By Wind and Word, and blurrèd Scheme—
    Oh, to stretch these narrow eyes, to dream!

Son of His Love

BEFRIEND him through the Son of his love.
The darkened heart, congealed in misery,
Cannot soak up that eternal light,
And soon its bleakest shadows seem all too bright,
Till the entire soul's in chancery,
And bound to repel the faintest gift thereof.
Befriend him!—through the Son of his love.

Goodness Knows

IT takes faith to wait,
Faith to believe in rewards to come,
That in the end all joy is ours,
To believe the good will hold.

It takes nothing to just let go,
Nothing to abandon all and lose control;
But still a bit of faith, when the nothing occurs,
To believe the good will hold.

Reunion

THE mountain down today to meet me,
And here am I, a far less perfect soul,
Out of place, yet home to its unassuming ease—
I cannot have for long this gentle breeze
Or claim my own this ancient, sacred dole.
The fog is lifted not by *my* command—
I wait for *God* to come and bless the land.
God, I think, will greet me.

The fire begs me to its flame,
Son of the father that peeks to break the morn,
Putting to rout the dew and the hollow's chilling air—
Uncle Joe is up and stirring there,
And in Aunt Gail the clan is daily born,
While the Mother—renewed—prays and reads aloud,
Bringing God again past hill and cloud,
This God before we came.

The creek I hear is out of time,
Yet speaks more of great, eternal streams
Than any stream of word that I, one man, can muster—
A reunion today of one remarkable cluster,
A holy history of spirited, fleshèd reams,
Apart but always near, unknown and known,
With God revealed in every bud and home—
God is ours! God is mine!

Up

SOME people
Fall for a time,
Others
For good.
I might get
Up again.
I have.
I could.

Leap

AFTER 12 she began to celebrate only on the 4,
    So by birth kept hope alive.
Foolish, her friends laughed, while admitting 64,
    That she claimed 25.

The End of Idealism

I ONCE allowed how all should be—
Now just how it is;
So surrenders bitter age,
Conceding wasted youth and rage.

All Wet

My best ideas come in the shower.
When the water roars upon my head,
It's all for me to think alone.
Notions, like the spray, cascade;
Ideas swirl and lather up the mind;
Eureka breaks through mist and fog.
I rush to finish what's left undone,
So eager am I for the towel.

But as the last few drops are drained,
As the clothes and shoes are on again,
All my wondrous thoughts are gone.
World peace, I think, is lost this way,
Diseases cured, the hungry fed.
The earth itself renewed in me—

If I could just dry out my head.

Culpability

UPON what precedent lies my guilt?
By what standard grade it?

Against the whole world, your offense,
And the Lord God who made it.

The Preener's Curse

AT least five minutes wasted
     In restraining seditious hair;
And three in search of soap
     With a scent he cares to share,
And two in rumination
     Of what effect he's had
If that old strain of deodorant
     Has unawares gone bad.

That's just ten minutes of a day
     To mark the preener's curse;
And curses me with far more time
     To write this sloppy verse.

To a Wanderer

CARA—

Think of me when you travel,
For somewhere in those Italian hills,
I am born.

On Growing Old

IT'S a comfort to know that as I fail,
    The universe does not,
That "cause and effect" continues to make sense,
    Despite the mystics' rot;
And the smoke coming from the kitchen
    Was my own false start:
Water and milk for some meal amiss,
    And the charring-bottomed pot!

It's a comfort to know that as I fail,
    Miracles still have a shot
Amidst this ordered, addled universe,
    Despite the pragmatists' rot;
And brewed its surprise this morning
    When java bean I sought:
Behold! black and brimming to the rim,
    Already in my pot!

Predate

I WILL love you in a past life,
    To that I vow.
We'll spend those days in breezy rapture,
    But it's not to be, not now.

About! turn back! by wise advice,
    So rue no harsh adieu,
For we will meet some yesterday,
    When care of now is through.

Listen, Love

CLOSE your eyes and listen, listen—
Silence hear the sound again—
All the realm is ours tonight,
At least till ten, at least till ten—
The doors are holding well and tight,
At least till ten, at least till ten;
Soon the chaos, soon the light,
But now, the calm, now the night.

Years Later

WHAT was I thinking? she wondered upon seeing him again.
How such a man could have fulfilled her girlhood fantasies
Was a mystery. A whiff of rosy happiness
Sought to engulf her and she shut it out. Right then
She remembered love again, and it seemed like madness.

Words of Love

WHAT you think of me is
    What I want to know—
For I gather only
    As your eyes may glow
In light of adoration;
    The yearning of love,
The sigh, the moan,
    Which in part makes love so.

I am a man,
    And a thinking man, too.
Such arrows thrill, yes,
    But never quite do;
I need more than song
    In the way of a love,
Than fire rekindled,
    Or hearts born anew.

This, then: talk—
    This is designed;
Talk, even as we've
    Enmeshed and aligned.
What you think of me—
    What I think of this love—
Sharing in body and
    And wholly of mind.

Alzheimer's

SHE was slowly overwhelmed by wind and sand,
Till all that once adorned the house—
The dabs of color, the splotches of cloth,
The photos of people they conjured together,
And all the fleeting trifles and trinkets
    Meant for happier times—
Were submerged by the merciless desert.

After some time he didn't recognize her,
But he pretended to, and sat nearby,
Taking shelter in dreams under the scorching sun,
While she watched him from deep within,
Silently, through a blasted window.

She is a Flower Garden

SHE is a flower garden,
Sweet with betony.
Her eyes are double daisies,
Her nose a peony.
Her mouth is scarlet tulip,
Her cheeks are jasmine fair,
And lacy mallow clusters
That grace the morning air.

She is a flower garden,
Spring-touched and summer-kissed.
She smiles at me with pansies,
Delights with love-in-a-mist.
"Foxglove" is her answer
Each time I call to her
(Sometimes more like "marjoram"
Or "linen's lavender").

She is a flower garden,
And I am at her gate.
Rows of frilly dianthus
Pretend it's not too late!
Sweet pea climbs above the rose
With pleasure's petal'd fare,

And I push past hydrangea
That I might enter there.

She is a flower garden
Of poppy and bleeding-heart,
And I will tend her in my thoughts
Long past the day we part.
And every bright chrysanthemum,
Or wood anemone,
Is reminiscent of our love,
The flower garden and me.

Distance

GROWING old means many things,
    But mostly this:
The work is done, the harvest over,
Time for moving on.

Instead they oft live backwards,
Holding on to roles long used up.
They cannot accept the plodding hour
That disunites hearts from their own—

Naturally, and much needed
    For closing in on God.

Friends Leave

"LET'S be friends," I posed—
"Friends leave," his pained reply.
"But I'm young—I will not leave you."
"And I'm old, and soon won't see you."

By a Thread, Gulping Life

I AM thinking of my mother tonight ...
Or of myself—which is it?
We are only miles apart, the two of us,
And miles of wires will expedite
A quick hello, or I may chose to visit
By car—it's not that far—and bless
Her with me and I with her, and thus
Recapture a bit of my boyish delight

At the mere sight of her smiling face;
And it is that face I am remembering now,
Which, in the dark of day and lonely night,
Has the power to overcome (but not erase)
The melancholy spirit that, somehow,
Paternally—marked or by roulette—
Stays on and swaggers and picks a fight ...
But then, by faith, by love, *her* grace

Recalled ... O God in Heaven above!
I thank you that upon my design,
You chose this vessel and not another,
In water and earthly home, whereof
I would grow, both human and divine,
Inspired of father and Father,
Bolstered by brother and brother,
But weaned at the breast of my mother,
Where I suckled—and swallowed—Love.

Mary Leapt Today

IN each time,
Against a bright and sunny clime,

Someone dear approaches the end,
As presaged by friend upon friend

Falling into what seems an abyss,
Which, sun or no, is hard to dismiss ...

But for faithful risers, the dawn will come,
Bringing hope that life cannot succumb

To the fearful clip of death;
That such grief is just a catch of breath

Before one moves on,
Skipping the chasm and into the dawn.

Mary leapt today.
Another's on her way.

Winter Message

OVERNIGHT the waters froze; winter had begun.
The geese, a-swim but days before, had rallied for the sun.
The shores at play just yesterday are turned and wrapped for sleep;
And frogs beneath the glassy pond are diving—dreaming—deep.

Not still! the pond objects aloud to proffered words like "glass."
Its quiet undulations preach a many-volumed past.
And so it sculpts the weasel's course, and so the beaver's trail;
And so in frozen, rippled words: His Spring can never fail.

Riversend

WHAT depths my soul will plummet when I'm gone!
What dreams to scale and sample when I'm down!
And no more silent mother, father, friend—
Children, meet me there at Riversend!
Find me near that cloud of great renown,
Among the many fated to this end.
Children, children,
> Come to Riversend!

Chance not this world to meet your bold desire,
For greater good is borne by something higher,
And sweeter voices hearts as these may mend—
Children, forget me not at Riversend!
Enjoy the world, but see above the mire,
And trust vicissitude, to this amend—
Children, children,
> Come to Riversend!

If not by lake or stream or fragrant tree,
In some dim hall of words I'm sure to be,
With all the worlds' redemptive truths to tend—
Children, come with me to Riversend!
Forever stunned by love and life to be—
Rejoice with us and nod unto this end!
Children, children, children—
> Riversend!